HEART-HEALTHY
everyday meals

dr jehanne ali

Marshall Cavendish
Cuisine

Series Designer: Bernard Go Kwang Meng

Published by Marshall Cavendish Cuisine
An imprint of Marshall Cavendish International

Other Marshall Cavendish Offices:
Marshall Cavendish Corporation. 99 White Plains Road, Tarrytown NY 10591-9001, USA • Marshall Cavendish International (Thailand) Co Ltd. 253 Asoke, 12th Flr, Sukhumvit 21 Road, Klongtoey Nua, Wattana, Bangkok 10110, Thailand • Marshall Cavendish (Malaysia) Sdn Bhd, Times Subang, Lot 46, Subang Hi-Tech Industrial Park, Batu Tiga, 40000 Shah Alam, Selangor Darul Ehsan, Malaysia

Marshall Cavendish is a trademark of Times Publishing Limited

National Library Board, Singapore Cataloguing-in-Publication Data

Ali, Jehanne.
Heart-healthy everyday meals / Dr Jehanne Ali. – Singapore : Marshall Cavendish Cuisine, [2013]
pages cm
ISBN : 978-981-4398-52-7 (paperback)

1. Heart – Diseases – Diet therapy – Recipes. 2. Cooking (Natural foods) 3. Cookbooks. I. Title. II. Series: Mini cookbooks.

TX714
641.56311 -- dc23   OCN829056896

Printed in Singapore by Saik Wah Print Media Pte Ltd

contents

HEART-HEALTHY
everyday meals

introduction

With cardiovascular diseases afflicting a growing number of people, it is essential that we scrutinise our lifestyle and do our best to maintain good health. Together with regular exercise and proper lifestyle management, a heart-healthy diet is pertinent to ensure that risk factors for heart diseases are eliminated. Specific conditions such as high blood pressure, adult onset diabetes and high cholesterol levels contribute directly to damaging blood vessels in the heart, which may lead to a heart attack and even sudden death. Diet, if managed poorly, can become a risk factor for heart diseases. What we need is a heart-healthy diet. We need foods that not only prevent the occurrence of high blood pressure, diabetes or high cholesterol levels, but superfoods that promote the well-being of the heart and possibly, repair the damage that was already done.

- *Consume foods that are rich in antioxidants regularly.*
  Berries such as strawberries, raspberries and blueberries are rich in natural antioxidants. Antioxidants prevent natural damage to the blood vessels and hence, in the long run, also help prevent formation of plaque in our coronaries. Tea, especially green tea, is a powerful antioxidant that has been scientifically proven to be able to promote longevity and improve overall well-being.
- *Incorporate the right amount of good fat in your diet.*
  Many have a misconception that fats are bad for health. While bad fats should be avoided, good fats like extra virgin olive oil, rapeseed or canola oil are now proven to be beneficial for the heart, and those are the oils that should be incorporated into our diet.
- *Eat the right kind of chocolate.*
  Moderation is key, and it is important to choose the right kind of chocolates to eat. Dark Chocolate is rich in antioxidants that prevent free radical formation, which damages heart vessels. The French Paradox diet theory recommends eating one small piece of chocolate with at least 56% cocoa a day to dramatically reduce the risk of heart diseases. A little tip: Eating citrus fruits with chocolate helps to increase the absorption of vitamins within the body.
- *Eat lots of fruits and vegetables.*
  Generally, all fruits and vegetables are good for you, but some are better than others. Pomegranate contains punicalagin, which is rich in antioxidants. Broccoli prevents free radical scavengers from damaging the coronaries. Tomatoes are chock-full of lycopene, which is good for the heart.

- *Eat more oily fish, and eat less red meat.*
  Oily fish such as salmon, tuna or mackerels are full of omega-3 fatty acids, and should be included at least three times a week in your diet.
- *Use herbs and spices to substitute salt and artificial flavourings.*
  Herbs such as parsley, thyme and oregano are so versatile and full of flavours, they not only enhance meals but also reduce the need for a higher amount of salt in the dish. Stay away from preservatives and flavourings such as monosodium glutamate. Spices such as turmeric, cayenne pepper, coriander and fennel are known to promote good health and prevent cancer. In fact, studies have shown that 2 Tbsp cayenne pepper can stop an ongoing heart attack, acting even faster than the recommended dose of aspirin!
- *Include legumes, beans and nuts in your diet.*
  There are just too many to choose from. To name a few, lentils, kidney beans, quinoa and chickpeas all contain fibres and minerals. The good news is, they are low in fat too.
- *Eat eggs in moderation.*
  Some health institutions advise that having one egg a day is good for maintaining overall well-being. It is alright to consume egg whites, but try to limit consumption of egg yolks to just two a day.

If you choose the right foods, you keep your body fit and your heart healthy. You can enjoy three delicious meals and even desserts too!

For more heart-healthy recipes, check out other books in this series with a heart-healthy theme: *Heart-healthy Soups & Stews*, *Heart-healthy Snacks* and *Heart-healthy Sweets & Desserts*.

acknowledgements

I would like to thank Audrey for this opportunity, as well as Le Creuset and WMF for their support and the products used in this book; my daughter Mishalle, for all the hours of baking fun and for being the real inspiration in our family; my husband, A for the unabated faith in me, you are my rock; my mother, for instilling in me the love for good food through her wonderful creations.

asyura Serves 12

Asyura is a healthy porridge of rice, vegetables and spices—a delicious and satisfying one-pot meal.

INGREDIENTS

Basmati rice	2 cups
Extra virgin olive oil	1 Tbsp
Red onions	2, peeled and finely sliced
Shallots	5, peeled and finely sliced
Ginger	2.5-cm (1-in) knob, peeled and minced
Garlic	3 cloves, peeled and minced
Beef	350 g (12$^1/_2$ oz), cut into small cubes
Coriander powder	2 Tbsp
Cumin powder	1 tsp
Cumin seeds	1 tsp
Ajwain (carom) seeds	1 tsp
Carrots	2, diced
Russet potatoes	3, washed, peeled and diced
Celery	1 stalk, cut into small cubes
Water	1.5 litres (48 fl oz / 6 cups)
Coriander leaves	1 packed cup, coarsely chopped
Ground black pepper	1 Tbsp
Salt	to taste

METHOD

• Soak the basmati rice for at least 30 minutes and drain off water.

• In a large casserole, heat olive oil and sauté onions, shallots, ginger and garlic until fragrant.

• Add beef and fry until brown.

• Add spices, carrots and potatoes and celery, followed by rice and water. Simmer on medium heat until rice is cooked and mushy.

• Season with pepper and salt. Add coriander leaves and give it a good stir.

• Garnish as desired and serve immediately.

roasted vegetable ciabatta Serves 6

Eggplants and courgettes contain antioxidants that help to prevent heart diseases. These ciabatta sandwiches are not only delicious, but also easy to prepare.

INGREDIENTS

Carrot	1, medium-sized, sliced lengthwise
Eggplant (aubergine/ brinjal)	1, sliced lengthwise
Red pepper (capsicum)	1, sliced lengthwise
Tomatoes	2, sliced
Courgette	1, sliced lengthwise
Shallots	2, peeled and finely sliced
Garlic	3 cloves, peeled and sliced
Oregano powder	1 Tbsp
Kosher salt	$1/2$ tsp + more for seasoning
Ground black pepper	1 tsp
Extra virgin olive oil	3 Tbsp + more for seasoning
Ciabatta rolls	6, sliced into halves

METHOD

- Preheat oven to 190°C (375°F).
- Place carrot, eggplant, red pepper, tomatoes and courgette on a roasting tray.
- Arrange shallots and garlic on top.
- Season with oregano, salt and black pepper. Drizzle olive oil over the ingredients.
- Roast vegetables for 35 minutes.
- Sandwich roasted vegetables in between two ciabatta halves.
- Season with salt and olive oil if desired.
- Serve immediately.

baked potato with carrot slaw Serves 2

Carrot slaw is used as a unique filling for these baked potatoes. This makes a healthy low fat meal which is nutritious and satisfying at the same time.

INGREDIENTS

Potatoes	2, large
Extra virgin olive oil	2 Tbsp
Kosher salt	to taste + more for slaw
Carrots	2, grated
Garlic	1 clove, peeled and minced
Shallot	1, peeled and finely sliced
Lemon juice and rind	from 1 lemon
Chilli flakes	$1/2$ tsp
Low fat plain Greek yoghurt	125 ml (4 fl oz / $1/2$ cup)
Parsley	4 Tbsp, finely chopped
Ground black pepper	1 Tbsp

METHOD

• Preheat oven to 190°C (375°F).

• Wash and pat dry potatoes.

• Make a cross slit on one side of the potato skin with a knife, then pierce each potato with a fork.

• Drizzle 1 Tbsp olive oil and sprinkle kosher salt.

• Wrap the potatoes in aluminium foil and bake for 35 minutes until tender.

• Meanwhile, prepare slaw. In a bowl, combine carrots, garlic, shallot, lemon juice and rind, chilli flakes, yoghurt, parsley, salt and pepper. Mix well and add remaining olive oil.

• When potatoes are ready, slice them lengthwise and serve with carrot slaw on top.

beef roast Serves 12

Curry is not always unhealthy. This Malabar-inspired dish combines fragrant spices with minimal oil without compromising the taste.

INGREDIENTS

Coriander powder	1 Tbsp
Cumin powder	1 Tbsp
Turmeric	1 tsp
Chilli powder	1 Tbsp
Beef fillet	1 kg (2 lb 3 oz), cut into small pieces
Ginger-garlic mix	2 Tbsp
Red onions	3, peeled and finely sliced
Curry leaves	a few sprigs + more for gravy
Water	500 ml (16 fl oz / 2 cups)
Canola oil	2 Tbsp
Shallots	3, peeled and finely sliced
Cinnamon stick	1
Cloves	3
Tomatoes	3, chopped
Salt	to taste
Cayenne pepper powder	1 tsp
Garam masala	1 Tbsp

N o T E

Ginger-garlic mix can be store-bought or homemade. To make your own, simply peel and mince an equal amount of ginger and garlic, then mix well.

METHOD

- Dry-roast coriander, cumin, turmeric and chilli powder in a hot pan until fragrant.

- Marinate beef with 1 Tbsp ginger-garlic mix, 1 red onion, the roasted spices and curry leaves. Refrigerate overnight or for at least 2 hours.

- Place marinated beef in a pressure cooker. Pour in water and pressure cook for 6 whistles. If using a normal casserole pot, simmer beef with water and cook for 45 minutes to 1 hour, until beef is tender (this generally takes a longer time).

- Prepare gravy. Heat oil in a frying pan. Temper curry leaves, shallots, 2 red onions, the remaining ginger-garlic mix, cinnamon and cloves.

- Add tomatoes and cook until mushy.

- Tip in cooked beef. Season with salt, cayenne pepper and garam masala.

- Simmer until gravy is dry.

- Serve warm with rice or bread.

black pepper beef and spinach stir-fry Serves 8

Moderate consumption of beef is good for health as it is a good source of iron. Combined with spinach, which is a heart-healthy vegetable, this aromatic stir-fry is full of flavour and nutrients.

INGREDIENTS

Beef or beef sukiyaki	500 g (1 lb 1 1/2 oz), thinly sliced
Ground black pepper	2 Tbsp
Light soy sauce	1 Tbsp
Oyster sauce	1 Tbsp
Salt	1/2 tsp + more for seasoning
Chilli flakes	1/2 tsp
Honey	1 Tbsp
Garlic	2 cloves, peeled and minced
Sesame oil	2 Tbsp
Red onion	1, peeled and sliced
Spinach leaves	1 packed cup

METHOD

- Marinate beef with black pepper, soy sauce, oyster sauce, salt, chilli flakes, honey and half of the minced garlic. Refrigerate for at least 1 hour or, preferably, overnight.

- Heat sesame oil in a wok. Once the wok is smoky, add marinated beef in batches and fry until brown. Set aside.

- Using the same oil, sauté remaining garlic and onion.

- Return beef to the wok. Add spinach and stir-fry.

- Once spinach has wilted, season with salt as desired and serve immediately.

prawn chap chye Serves 6–8

This oriental delight can be served as a side dish for main meals.

INGREDIENTS

Glass noodles	$^1/_4$ cup
Sesame oil	2 Tbsp
King prawns	800 g (1$^3/_4$ lb), shelled and deveined
Red chillies	2, sliced
Red onion	1, peeled and quartered
Garlic	2 cloves, peeled and diced
Ginger	2.5-cm (1-in) knob, peeled and grated
Broccoli	2 heads, chopped
Carrots	2, cut into strips
Red pepper (capsicum)	1, diced
Yellow pepper (capsicum)	1, diced
Ground black pepper	1 tsp
Dark soy sauce	1 Tbsp
Oyster sauce	1 Tbsp
Corn flour (cornstarch)	1 Tbsp
Salt	to taste

METHOD

• Soak the glass noodles in warm water until they are soft.

• Meanwhile, heat sesame oil in a wok and sauté the prawns until pink. Set aside.

• Using the same oil, sauté the red chillies, onion and garlic until fragrant. Add ginger and fry for few more minutes.

• Throw in broccoli, carrots, red and yellow peppers, black pepper, followed by soy sauce and oyster sauce.

• Return prawns to the work and mix well.

• Combine corn flour with few tablespoons of water to form a paste. Pour mixture into the wok to thicken the gravy.

• Season with salt and remove from heat. Serve immediately.

chicken caesar salad Serves 2

Chicken Caesar salad is traditionally made with anchovies and rich dressing. Try this healthier version using good fat such as olive oil, and bake the chicken and croutons instead of frying them.

INGREDIENTS

Chicken breast fillet	280 g (10 oz)
Salt	$^1/_4$ tsp
Ground black pepper	$^1/_2$ tsp
Honey	1 tsp
Paprika	1 Tbsp
Wholemeal bread	1 slice
Oregano powder	1 tsp
Extra virgin olive oil	1 Tbsp

SALAD

Iceberg lettuce	1 cup
Red onion	1, peeled and quartered
Hard boiled egg	1, halved
Cucumber	1, sliced
Cherry tomatoes	a handful
Salt	to taste
Ground black pepper	to taste
Extra virgin olive oil	2 Tbsp

DRESSING

Extra virgin olive oil	4 Tbsp
Light mayonnaise	3 Tbsp
Dijon mustard	1 Tbsp
Vinegar	4 Tbsp
Parmesan cheese	1 Tbsp, grated
Salt	a pinch

METHOD

- Marinate chicken with salt, black pepper, honey and paprika for a few hours or overnight.

- Preheat oven to 180°C (350°F).

- Cut bread into cubes and mix well with oregano and 1 Tbsp olive oil. Place onto a baking tray.

- Wrap chicken in a foil and place on the same baking tray. Bake for 20 minutes.

- Once cooled, shred chicken and toss into a salad bowl.

- Add baked croutons and salad ingredients into salad bowl.

- Prepare dressing. Mix all the ingredients in a mason jar. Cover with lid and shake to emulsify.

- Drizzle minimal amount of dressing onto the salad. Mix well and serve.

chicken sambal Serves 4

A traditional Asian fare, sambal is popular all across Southeast Asia and beyond. This recipe uses less oil and includes turmeric. Turmeric contains curcumin, which prevents aging and damage to heart cells.

INGREDIENTS

Chicken with bones	800 g ($1^3/_4$ lb), cut into pieces
Ground black pepper	1 Tbsp
Turmeric	1 tsp
Salt	to taste + more for seasoning
Dried red chillies	10
Garlic	3 cloves, peeled
Red onions	2, peeled and sliced
Shrimp paste (belacan)	$^1/_2$ tsp
Tamarind pulp	1 Tbsp
Canola oil	1 Tbsp
Brown sugar	2 Tbsp

METHOD

• Wash chicken pieces and marinate with black pepper, turmeric and salt for 1 hour.

• Steam chicken until tender, then grill for 8 minutes at 200°C (400°F).

• Soak red chillies in hot boiling water for 10 minutes.

• Blend softened chillies with garlic, 1 onion, shrimp paste and tamarind pulp to form a smooth paste.

• Heat oil in a wok and sauté remaining onion slices.

• Add red chilli paste and fry until the oil splutters.

• Season with brown sugar and salt.

• As the paste thickens, add chicken pieces and coat well with paste.

• Remove from heat and serve.

healthy chicken korma Serves 8

A medley of spices, which have anti-inflammatory properties, are used in this dish. This traditional korma recipe is tweaked to create a healthier delicious meal.

INGREDIENTS

Whole chicken	1, cut into pieces
Salt	$1/2$ tsp + more for seasoning
Turmeric	1 tsp
Paprika	1 Tbsp
Canola oil	2 Tbsp
Red onions	2, peeled and sliced
Tomato	1, sliced
Red pepper (capsicum)	1, sliced
Coriander powder	2 Tbsp
Curry powder	1 Tbsp
Low fat plain yoghurt	125 ml (4 fl oz / $1/2$ cup)
Almonds	$1/4$ cup
Ground black pepper	1 tsp
Coriander leaves	a handful
Fresh basil leaves	a handful

METHOD

• Marinate chicken pieces with salt, turmeric and paprika for 30 minutes.

• Preheat oven to 180°C (350°F).

• In a hot wok, heat oil and pan-fry chicken until half cooked. Remove chicken from heat and leave oil in the wok.

• Using same oil, sauté onions, tomato and red pepper.

• In a blender, process coriander powder, curry powder, turmeric, yoghurt and almond with a dash of water to form a thick paste.

- Add paste to the wok and simmer on low heat.

- Season gravy with black pepper and salt.

- Place chicken on a baking tray and pour gravy on top.

- Bake for 25 minutes, until chicken is tender and gravy has thickened.

- Sprinkle coriander leaves and basil leaves on top.

- Serve warm.

corn flakes chicken Serves 2–4

Chicken breast is low in fat and cholesterol. Served with crunchy corn flakes crumbs, this baked chicken dish is healthy and delicious at the same time.

INGREDIENTS

Chicken breast fillets	2, about 200 g (7 oz) each
Ginger-garlic mix (see page 16)	1 tsp
Salt	1/2 tsp
Extra virgin olive oil	1 Tbsp
Red chilli flakes	1 tsp
Corn flakes	1 cup, crushed
Cayenne pepper powder	1 Tbsp
Oregano powder	1 tsp
Egg	1, beaten

METHOD

- Wash chicken breast and make few slits along the fillet with a knife.
- Marinate chicken with ginger-garlic mix, salt, olive oil and chilli flakes for 30 minutes.
- Preheat oven to 180°C (350°F).
- In a bowl, combine corn flakes with cayenne pepper and oregano.
- Pour beaten egg in a bowl or shallow dish.
- Immerse chicken breast in egg, then coat with corn flake mix.
- Place chicken fillets on a baking tray. Bake for 25 minutes or until golden brown and crispy.
- Slice before serving.

sweet potato cottage pie Serves 8

Sweet potatoes are healthier than regular potatoes, and this traditional dish is tweaked to include vegetables and chicken mince, which is low in fat.

INGREDIENTS

Sweet potatoes	600 g (1 lb 5²/₅ oz), washed
Cheddar cheese	100 g (3¹/₂ oz), grated
Skimmed milk	4 Tbsp
Extra virgin olive oil	1 Tbsp
Red onion	1, peeled and chopped
Cinnamon stick	1
Garlic	2 cloves, peeled and minced
Chicken mince	500 g (1 lb 1¹/₂ oz)
Tomatoes	200 g (7 oz), chopped
Garden peas	150 g (5¹/₃ oz)
Carrot	1, coarsely chopped
French green beans	a few stalks, finely chopped
Paprika	2 Tbsp
Cumin powder	1 tsp
Italian seasoning	1 Tbsp
Ground black pepper	1 Tbsp
Kosher salt	¹/₂ tsp

METHOD

- Boil sweet potatoes until tender. Mash in a mixing bowl and add cheese and milk. Mix well.
- Preheat oven to 180°C (350°F).
- Heat olive oil in a pan. Sauté onion, cinnamon stick and garlic until tender, then add chicken mince. Once meat is almost white, add tomatoes and vegetables.
- Simmer on low heat. Add paprika, cumin powder, Italian seasoning, black pepper and salt.
- Transfer onto a shallow baking dish and spoon mashed sweet potatoes on top.
- Bake for 30 minutes, until the top is golden brown.
- Serve immediately.

feta, olive and courgette salad Serves 4

This is a perfect cooling salad on a hot summer day, refreshing and healthy with the addition of olives and a drizzle of olive oil.

INGREDIENTS

Courgettes	2
Spring onion (scallion)	1 stalk, finely sliced
Black olives	$^1/_2$ cup, pitted
Feta cheese	$^3/_4$ packed cup, cubed
Extra virgin olive oil	3 Tbsp
Lemon juice	from 1 lemon
Garlic	2 cloves, peeled and minced
Kosher salt	$^1/_2$ tsp
Chilli flakes	1 tsp
Oregano powder	1 tsp

METHOD

- Using a mandoline, shave courgette into long ribbons.
- In a bowl, mix courgette ribbons with spring onion, black olives and feta cheese.
- Prepare dressing in a small bowl. Whisk olive oil with lemon juice, garlic, salt, chilli flakes and oregano.
- Drizzle dressing onto salad and serve.

black pepper and herb crusted salmon Serves 2

This delicious salmon dish is fuss-free and can be prepared in no time at all.

INGREDIENTS

Salmon fillets	2, about 140 g (5 oz) each
Garlic	2 cloves, peeled and minced
Ginger	1 tsp, peeled and minced
Ground black pepper	2 Tbsp
Oregano powder	2 tsp
Cayenne pepper powder	2 tsp
Chilli flakes	2 tsp
Kosher salt	1 tsp
Lemon juice	from 1 lemon
Extra virgin olive oil	2 Tbsp
Asparagus spears	6–8

METHOD

• Marinate salmon with all the other ingredients for at least 1 hour.

• Grease the pan with olive oil and pan-fry salmon until both sides are cooked. Remove from heat and transfer onto serving plates.

• Garnish as desired with asparagus spears or a salad. Serve immediately.

breakfast granola Makes 1 big jar

Daily consumption of oats can dramatically reduce the risk of heart disease.

INGREDIENTS

Extra virgin olive oil	250 ml (8 fl oz / 1 cup)
Dark brown sugar	1 cup
Water	125 ml (4 fl oz / $^{1}/_{2}$ cup)
Kosher salt	$^{1}/_{2}$ tsp
Cinnamon powder	1 Tbsp
Rolled oats	4 cups
Almonds	1 cup, chopped
Desiccated coconut	$^{1}/_{2}$ cup
Dried figs	$^{1}/_{2}$ cup
Sultanas	1 cup
Dark chocolate chips	$^{1}/_{2}$ cup

METHOD

• Preheat oven to 180°C (350°F).

• In a saucepan, combine olive oil, brown sugar, water, salt and cinnamon.

• Simmer on low heat until sugar is melted and bubbling.

• Meanwhile, in a mixing bowl, combine rolled oats with almonds, coconut and dried figs. Pour hot oil mixture into the bowl and mix well.

• Spread the oats in clusters on a greased baking tray. Bake for 25 minutes, turning the tray once halfway through the baking.

• Remove from oven and add sultanas and chocolate chips. Mix well.

• Once cooled, store in an airtight container.

chicken and green lentil brown rice Serves 6

Lentils are high in protein and good for the heart. Omit chicken for a vegetarian version.

INGREDIENTS

Coriander powder	1 Tbsp
Turmeric	$^1/_2$ tsp
Cumin powder	1 tsp
Paprika	1 tsp
Extra virgin olive oil	3 Tbsp
Cinnamon stick	1
Cloves	3
Shallots	3, peeled and diced
Red chilli	1, finely chopped
Ginger-garlic mix (see page 16)	1 tsp
Chicken breast fillet	1, about 200 g (7 oz), cubed
Chickpeas	$^1/_2$ cup
Green lentils	$^3/_4$ cup, soaked for 2 hours
Brown rice	1 cup, washed and drained
Salt	to season
Coriander leaves	$^1/_2$ cup + more for garnishing
Parsley leaves	3 Tbsp, chopped
Water	750 ml (24 fl oz / 3 cups)

METHOD

- Prepare spice mix. In a small bowl, mix coriander powder, turmeric, cumin powder and paprika with 2 Tbsp water. Set aside.

- Heat olive oil in a dutch oven. Temper cinnamon stick and cloves until fragrant.

- Fry shallots, red chilli and ginger-garlic mix until golden brown.

- Add chicken cubes and spice mix. Coat chicken cubes well with spices and cook for around 10 minutes, until they are almost golden.

- Add chickpeas, green lentils and brown rice. Season with salt. Once all the ingredients are well combined, splutter coriander and parsley leaves on top, then pour in water. Cook over medium heat until water is absorbed and rice is thoroughly cooked.

- Garnish with coriander leaves and serve.

mee goreng mamak Serves 8

Mee Goreng Mamak is popular across Malaysia and Singapore. This version is healthier with the use of minimal oil and the addition of bean curd and spinach. You can now enjoy the authentic delicious taste of Mee Goreng Mamak without feeling guilty!

INGREDIENTS

Dried red chillies	8, soaked in hot water until soft
Shallots	3, peeled
Red onions	2, peeled
Garlic	2 cloves, peeled
Shrimp paste (*belacan*)	1 tsp
Canola oil	2 Tbsp
Firm bean curd	100 g (3$^1/_2$ oz), cubed
Tomatoes	2, large
Dark soy sauce	1 Tbsp
Tomato ketchup	1 Tbsp
Eggs	3, beaten
Egg noodles	400 g (14 oz)
Spinach leaves	1 packed cup, coarsely chopped
Salt	to taste

METHOD

- Place chillies, shallots, onions, garlic and shrimp paste in a blender. Add just enough water and blend to form a thick paste.

- Heat oil in a wok and fry bean curd cubes.

- Add blended spices and temper until the oil splutters.

- Add tomatoes, soy sauce and ketchup. Cook until mushy.

- Add beaten eggs, scrambling as they are being cooked.

- Tip in noodles, followed by spinach and salt.

- Once spinach has wilted and the noodles are semi-dry, remove from heat and serve.

fruity berry oatmeal porridge Serves 4

Oats can dramatically reduce total cholesterol level, regulate blood glucose and prevent heart diseases. It is so good that I totally recommend oatmeal for breakfast every day.

INGREDIENTS

Rolled oats	1 cup
Low fat milk	250 ml (8 fl oz / 1 cup)
Water	250 ml (8 fl oz / 1 cup)
Sultanas	4 Tbsp
Salt	a pinch
Honey	1 tsp + more to taste
Almonds	2 Tbsp, chopped and slightly toasted
Mixed berries (blueberries, strawberries and raspberries)	1 cup

METHOD

- Soak oats in milk for 10 minutes or, preferably, overnight in the fridge.

- Place soaked oats without the milk, water and sultanas in a heated saucepan. Lastly, pour in milk.

- Simmer on low heat and keep stirring for about 10 minutes, until oats are cooked.

- Add salt, honey and toasted almonds. Turn off heat.

- Put the lid on and leave the porridge to cool for 10 minutes on the stove.

- Divide porridge into bowls and serve with mixed berries. Drizzle honey over porridge if desired.

prawn tagliatelle with basil pesto Serves 8

This Mediterranean-inspired dish features olive oil and basil as the main ingredients. Light and flavourful, it makes a satisfying meal.

INGREDIENTS

Jumbo king prawns	500 g (1 lb 1 1/2 oz), washed
Paprika	1 tsp
Tagliatelle	300 g (10 1/2 oz)
Basil leaves	2 cups
Extra virgin olive oil	4 Tbsp
Pecorino Romano or Parmesan cheese	5 x 5-cm (2 x 2-in) block
Garlic	2 cloves, peeled + 1 tsp minced
Pine nuts	1/2 cup
Kosher salt	1 tsp
Olive oil	1 Tbsp
Chilli flakes	1 Tbsp
Lemon juice	from 1 lemon
Ground black pepper	1 tsp

METHOD

• Marinate prawns with paprika for about 30 minutes.

• Cook tagliatelle according to package instructions, until almost al dente. Drain and set aside.

• Prepare basil pesto. Using a mortar and pestle or a blender, process basil leaves with extra virgin olive oil, cheese, 2 cloves garlic, pine nuts and salt until smooth.

• Heat olive oil in a wok and sauté 1 tsp minced garlic.

• Throw in marinated prawns until pan-fry until they turn pink.

• Add chilli flakes, lemon juice and 4 Tbsp basil pesto.

• Once well combined, remove from heat and mix in tagliatelle.

• Coat tagliatelle well with pesto and spices. Allow the heat from the wok to cook the tagliatelle further, until al dente.

• Season with black pepper and serve warm.

potato frittata Serves 6

Frittatas are flavourful and easy to prepare. Eggs, when consumed in moderation, are good for the heart. Combined with spices that have anti-inflammatory properties, this recipe promises a healthy and tasty meal.

INGREDIENTS

Eggs	6, large
Skimmed milk	4 Tbsp
Ground black pepper	1 tsp
Chilli flakes	1 tsp
Kosher salt	$^1/_2$ tsp
Extra virgin olive oil	2 Tbsp
Russet potatoes	2, washed, peeled and finely sliced
Red onion	1, peeled and sliced
Garlic	2 cloves, peeled and minced
Tomato	1, diced
Coriander leaves	$^1/_2$ cup, coarsely chopped + more for garnishing
Oregano powder	1 tsp

METHOD

• Whisk eggs, milk, black pepper, chilli flakes and salt until frothy. Set aside.

• On a skillet, heat olive oil and pan fry potatoes until almost brown. Set aside.

• Preheat oven to 180°C (350°F).

• Using the same oil, sauté onion slices, garlic and tomato briefly.

• Add half of the potatoes, followed by coriander.

• Gently pour in egg mixture. Arrange remaining potato slices on top and sprinkle oregano powder over.

• Cook on low heat for 10 minutes.

• Transfer the skillet into the oven and bake for 15 minutes.

• Garnish with coriander leaves and serve immediately.

red onion and mushroom pizza Makes one 20-cm (8-in) pizza

The classic pizza gets a healthy revamp by omitting cheese altogether without compromising the taste. This is perfect for a vegetarian meal, bursting with the rich flavours of mushrooms, red onions and tangy tomatoes.

INGREDIENTS

PIZZA DOUGH

Bread flour	170 g (6 oz)
Instant yeast	1 tsp
Sugar	$^1/_4$ tsp
Extra virgin olive oil	3 Tbsp
Salt	$^1/_2$ tsp
Warm water	180 ml (6 fl oz / $^3/_4$ cup) or as required

TOPPING

Extra virgin olive oil	2 Tbsp
Garlic	1 clove, peeled and minced
Tomatoes	3, finely chopped
Oregano powder	1 Tbsp
Salt	to taste
Ground black pepper	to taste
Red onions	2, peeled and finely sliced
Button mushrooms	1 cup, finely sliced
Italian seasoning	1 Tbsp

METHOD

- Prepare pizza dough. Combine bread flour, yeast, sugar, olive oil and salt in a bowl.
- Add warm water gradually whilst kneading, until soft elastic dough is formed. Note that the gluten content varies across different brands of flours, so adjust the amount of water as needed.
- Leave dough to rise for about 1 hour, until it has doubled in volume.
- Prepare topping. Heat olive oil in a pan and sauté garlic until fragrant.
- Add tomatoes and cook until they are really mushy.

- Season with oregano, salt and black pepper.

- Preheat oven to 200°C (400°F).

- Once dough has risen, punch dough down. Using oiled hands, shape dough into a circular pizza base of 20 cm (8 in) in diameter.

- Spoon cooked tomatoes on top. Sprinkle onions and mushrooms over.

- Drizzle Italian seasoning over and place on a pizza stone or greased baking tray. Bake for 15–18 minutes.

- Garnish as desired and serve immediately.

49

spinach tagliatelle with herbs and quail eggs Serves 6

For its rich flavour, this dish is surprisingly easy to make. Research has shown that quail eggs provide many nutritional benefits, which include the ability to reduce the risks of heart diseases and cancer.

INGREDIENTS

Spinach tagliatelle	400 g (14 oz)
Garlic	2 cloves, peeled and minced
Parsley	4 Tbsp, finely chopped
Thyme	a few sprigs
Oregano powder	1 Tbsp
Cayenne pepper powder	1 tsp
Lemon juice	from 1 lemon
Extra virgin olive oil	3 Tbsp
Kosher salt	1 tsp
Quail eggs	10, hard-boiled, halved
Pecorino Romano or Parmesan cheese (optional)	to taste, grated

METHOD

- Cook spinach tagliatelle according to package instructions until al dente.
- Prepare pasta dressing. In a bowl, combine garlic, parsley, thyme, oregano, cayenne pepper, lemon juice and olive oil. Season with salt and drizzle on the cooked pasta.
- Top with quail eggs.
- Garnish with cheese if desired. Serve immediately.

prawn masala Serves 6

Serve this fuss-free dish for a quick, healthy weeknight meal.

INGREDIENTS

Canola oil	2 Tbsp
Curry leaves	a few sprigs
Red chilli	1, sliced
Grated coconut	4 Tbsp
Fenugreek seeds	$1/4$ tsp
Red onions	2, peeled and finely sliced
Shallots	2, peeled and finely sliced
Ginger-garlic mix (see page 16)	2 Tbsp
Tomatoes	2, large, chopped
Jumbo king prawns	1 kg (2 lb 3 oz), washed
Chilli powder	1 Tbsp
Tamarind paste	1 Tbsp
Turmeric	1 tsp
Cumin powder	1 tsp
Salt	a pinch

METHOD

- In a hot wok, heat oil and temper curry leaves, chilli, coconut and fenugreek seeds.
- Add onions, shallots and ginger-garlic mix. Sauté until fragrant.
- Tip in tomatoes and cook until they are mushy.
- Add prawns followed by chilli powder, tamarind, turmeric and cumin powder.
- Season with just a pinch of salt, and remove from heat once the prawns have turned pink.
- Serve warm with steamed rice or bread.

chicken spinach quesadilla Serves 2

This recipe uses minimal cheese and white meat. Low in fat yet savoury, this Mexican dish makes a satisfying and nutritious meal.

INGREDIENTS

Extra virgin olive oil	2 Tbsp
Onion	1, peeled and diced
Garlic	2–3 cloves, peeled and crushed
Chicken breast fillet	about 280 g (10 oz), cut into small cubes
Paprika	$^1/_2$ tsp
Chilli flakes	1 Tbsp
Cayenne pepper powder	1 Tbsp
Cumin powder	1 tsp
Lemon juice	from 1 lemon
Coarse sea salt	$^1/_2$ tsp
Spinach leaves	a handful
Tortilla wraps	2
Low fat Cheddar and Mozzarella cheese	4 Tbsp, grated

METHOD

• Heat olive oil in a wok. Stir-fry onion and crushed garlic.

• Add chicken cubes and stir-fry until chicken has browned.

• Add paprika, chilli flakes, cayenne pepper, cumin, lemon juice and sea salt. When chicken is almost dry and well-coated with spices, add spinach and turn off heat.

• Divide chicken cubes between 2 tortilla wraps. Sprinkle cheese over and fold the wraps close.

• Grill tortilla wraps for 4–5 minutes on each side, until both sides are golden brown and the cheese has melted.

• Serve immediately.

ratatouille Serves 4

This classic French dish is low in fat and high in antioxidants. Its main ingredients are purely vegetables, but the taste is robust even without the addition of meat.

INGREDIENTS

Extra virgin olive oil	2 Tbsp
Red onion	1, peeled and sliced
Shallots	2, peeled and sliced
Garlic	2 cloves, peeled and minced
Red chilli	1, sliced
Eggplant (aubergine/ brinjal)	1, cubed
Courgette	1, cubed
Tomatoes	2, cubed
Cherry tomatoes	$1/2$ cup, halved
Red pepper (capsicum)	1, cubed
Bay leaf	1
Basil leaves	a handful
Balsamic vinegar	2 Tbsp
Honey	1 Tbsp
Salt	to taste
Ground black pepper	to taste
Oregano powder	1 tsp

METHOD

- Heat olive oil in a casserole. Sauté onion, shallots and garlic until fragrant.
- Add chilli, eggplant, courgette, tomatoes and red pepper. Mix in bay leaf and basil leaves, followed by balsamic vinegar and honey.
- Simmer on low heat until the vegetables are cooked, with the lid on.
- Season with salt, pepper and oregano.
- Serve as a side dish with rice, or enjoy with a baguette or wholemeal leavened bread.

herb-roasted chicken with stuffing Serves 8

Roast chicken is always a winner for elaborate family dinners. Try out this roast, which is not only low in fat but also deliciously flavourful.

INGREDIENTS

Whole chicken	1, about 2 kg (4 lb 6 oz), skinned and washed
Salt	1 Tbsp
Ground black pepper	1 Tbsp
Olive oil	4 Tbsp
Honey	3 Tbsp
Garlic	3 cloves, peeled and minced
Paprika	1 tsp
Dried Italian seasoning	1 tsp
Thyme	a few sprigs
Rosemary	a few sprigs

CASHEW HERB STUFFING

Extra virgin olive oil	3 Tbsp
Red onion	1, peeled and minced
Garlic	2 cloves, peeled and minced
Cashew nuts	4 Tbsp, coarsely chopped
Breadcrumbs	1/2 cup
Thyme	a few springs
Rosemary	a few springs
Lemon zest	from 1 lemon
Sage leaves	a few
Parsley	a few springs
Salt	to taste
Ground black pepper	to taste

METHOD

- Marinate chicken with all ingredients except those under the cashew herb stuffing. Leave for at least for 2 hours or, ideally, overnight.

- Preheat oven to 180°C (350°F).

- Prepare cashew herb stuffing. In a saucepan, heat olive oil and tip in all the ingredients.

- Pan-fry for few minutes. Stuff mixture into chicken.

- Roast chicken for 35 minutes or until it is golden brown.

- Serve immediately.

salmon en papillote Serves 2

Salmon is rich in omega-3 fatty acids, which can boost heart health and reduce the risk of inflammation. This recipe shows how you can prepare salmon the healthier way without compromising on taste.

INGREDIENTS

Salmon steaks	2, about 225 g (8 oz) each
Red onion	1, peeled and sliced
Cherry tomatoes	$^1/_2$ cup, halved
Cayenne pepper powder	1 Tbsp
Extra virgin olive oil	2 Tbsp
Oregano powder	1 tsp
Lemon juice	from 1 lemon
Kosher salt	$^1/_2$ tsp
Ground black pepper	1 tsp
Parsley	a few sprigs
Coriander leaves	a few sprigs

METHOD

• Preheat oven to 180°C (350°F).

• Wash salmon steaks. Place each steak on a piece of parchment paper large enough to enclose it.

• In a bowl, mix the rest of the ingredients except parsley and coriander leaves.

• Coat salmon steaks with mixture. Top with parsley and coriander leaves.

• Fold or staple the edges of the parchment paper so that the contents are securely wrapped.

• Bake for 25 minutes.

• Serve warm, with salads, potatoes, or steamed rice if desired.

tuna and rocket salad sandwich Serves 4

Like salmon, tuna is a good source of omega-3 fatty acids, and can be included about three times a week in our diet.

INGREDIENTS

Store-bought tuna in brine	1 can
Chilli flakes	1 tsp
Sweetcorn kernels	$1/2$ cup
Lemon juice	from 1 lemon
Salt	a pinch
Olive oil	$1/2$ tsp
Butter	to taste
Wholemeal bread	8 slices
Rocket leaves	1 cup

METHOD

- In a bowl, combine tuna with chilli flakes, sweetcorn, lemon juice, salt and olive oil.
- Spread some butter on bread slices and spread tuna mixture over.
- Garnish with rocket leaves and top with another slice of bread.
- Cut diagonally and serve.

spaghetti with spicy chicken meatballs Serves 6

This is a popular favourite for all ages. Healthy and hearty, it makes a great meal for toddlers too.

INGREDIENTS

Spaghetti	400 g (14 oz)
Extra virgin olive oil	3 Tbsp
Garlic	3 cloves, peeled and minced
Canned tomatoes	1 can
Bay leaves	a few
Italian seasoning	1 Tbsp
Salt	to taste
Ground black pepper	to taste

CHICKEN MEATBALLS

Olive oil	for pan-frying
Chicken mince	600 g (1 lb 5²/₅ oz)
Ginger-garlic mix (see page 16)	1 Tbsp
Plain (all-purpose) flour	1 Tbsp
Onion	1, peeled and finely chopped
Coriander powder	1 Tbsp
Paprika	1 tsp
Cumin powder	1 tsp
Tomato ketchup	1 Tbsp
Oregano powder	1 tsp
Salt	1 tsp
Eggs	2

METHOD

- Prepare chicken meatballs. In a bowl, combine all ingredients except olive oil.
- Heat olive oil in a pan.
- Form meatballs of about 2 cm (1 in) in diameter and pan-fry in heated oil until almost brown. Remove from heat and set aside.
- In a separate pot, cook the spaghetti until al dente. Drain and set aside.

- Heat olive oil in a casserole and sauté garlic.
- Add tomatoes and cook for a few minutes until tomatoes are mushy.
- Add meatballs, bay leaves, Italian seasoning, salt and pepper.
- Simmer on low heat with minimal stirring until gravy has thickened.
- Serve immediately with spaghetti.

omato penne Serves 6

his classic dish brings out the best flavours of tomatoes and herbs. The sauce can be kept
•frigerated for later use.

INGREDIENTS

Penne	300 g (10½ oz)
Extra virgin olive oil	3 Tbsp
Garlic	3 cloves, peeled and minced
Paprika	1 Tbsp
Fresh tomatoes	2, coarsely chopped
Canned tomatoes	400 g (14 oz)
Passata	200 ml (6¾ fl oz)
Bay leaf	1
Oregano powder	1 tsp
Ground black pepper	1 Tbsp
Kosher salt	1 tsp
Parmesan shavings	to taste

NOTE
Passata is liquid tomato purée. It can be bought from supermarkets. Alternatively, you can make your own passata by passing fresh or canned tomatoes through a sieve. The liquid collected is ready for use immediately.

METHOD

- Cook penne according to package instructions, until al dente. Drain and set aside.
- Heat olive oil in a pan and sauté garlic.
- Add paprika and both fresh and canned tomatoes. Cook until they are mushy.
- Tip in passata, bay leaf, oregano, black pepper and salt.
- Simmer on low heat until gravy is thick and glossy.
- Spoon gravy over penne. Garnish with Parmesan shavings and serve.

tuna niçoise salad Serves 4

Packed with the goodness of tuna, vegetables and tomatoes, this salad is a healthy treat that is jazzed up with a delicious dressing.

INGREDIENTS

SALAD

Store-bought tuna in brine	1 can
Red onion	1, peeled and quartered
Hard boiled eggs	2, halved
Anchovy fillets	3–4, cut into long strips
Cherry tomatoes	$1/2$ cup, halved
Baby potatoes	3, boiled and halved
Parsley	4 Tbsp, chopped
Romaine lettuce	4–6 leaves, coarsely chopped

DRESSING

Extra virgin olive oil	4 Tbsp
Dijon mustard	1 tsp
Lemon juice	from 1 lemon
Salt	$1/2$ tsp
Ground black pepper	$1/2$ tsp
Honey	2 Tbsp
Oregano powder	1 tsp
Chilli flakes	$1/2$ tsp
Garlic	1 clove, peeled and minced

METHOD

- Mix all the salad ingredients in a salad bowl.
- Whisk all dressing ingredients in a separate bowl until well combined.
- Drizzle dressing onto salad and serve immediately.

vegetable pilaf Serves 6

Not all flavoured rice are fattening. In fact, this pilaf can be eaten often, as it is full of vegetables and cooked with olive oil, which contains good fat.

INGREDIENTS

Extra virgin olive oil	3 Tbsp
Curry leaves	a few sprigs
Cinnamon stick	1
Cumin seeds	1 tsp
Cloves	2
Star anise	2
Ginger-garlic mix (see page 16)	1 Tbsp
Red onions	2, peeled and finely sliced
Coriander powder	1 Tbsp
Turmeric	1 tsp
Cayenne pepper powder	1 tsp
Bay leaf	1
Ground black pepper	1 tsp
Frozen mixed vegetables	2 cups, thawed
Basmati rice	3 cups, washed
Saffron threads	a few strands, soaked in 3–4 Tbsp rose water or water
Water	1.5 litres (48 fl oz / 6 cups)
Salt	1 tsp

METHOD

- Heat olive oil in a wok and temper curry leaves, cinnamon stick, cumin seeds, cloves and star anise until fragrant.
- Add ginger-garlic mix and onions. Fry until onions are translucent.
- Add coriander powder, turmeric, cayenne pepper, bay leaf and black pepper.
- Tip in mixed vegetables and stir to mix well.

- Add basmati rice and stir so the rice grains are well coated with spices and evenly mixed with vegetables.

- Pour in saffron mixture.

- Transfer into a rice cooker and add water and salt.

- When rice is cooked, fluff it up with a fork.

- Serve warm, with gravy or salads if desired.

black bean burger Serves 8

This is a healthy alternative to take-out burgers. Black beans are inexpensive, and is not only nutritious but also tasty.

INGREDIENTS

Black beans	1 cup, soaked in water overnight
Onion	1, peeled and finely diced
Garlic	1 clove, peeled and minced
Paprika	1 tsp
Cumin powder	1 tsp
Red pepper (capsicum)	1, cut into small cubes
Corn kernels	$1/2$ cup
Salt	$1/2$ tsp
Ground black pepper	1 tsp
Egg	1, beaten
Breadcrumbs	$1/2$ cup
Olive oil	for pan-frying
Burger buns	8, halved
Tomato slices	as desired
Iceberg lettuce	as desired
Garlic sauce	to taste

METHOD

- Boil black beans in hot water with a pinch of salt until tender.

- Drain off the water and mash beans in a large mixing bowl.

- Combine mashed beans with diced onion, garlic, paprika, cumin, red pepper, corn, salt and black pepper.

- Once well mixed, add egg and breadcrumbs to form a sticky dough.

- Using clean hands, form flat patties from the dough.

- Lightly coat a skillet with just enough olive oil to grease it. When heated, pan-fry the patties until both sides are golden brown.

- Place a patty on each half of a burger bun. Garnish with tomato slices, lettuce and garlic sauce. Cover with top halves of burgers. Serve immediately.

fishball noodle soup Serves 4

A light and savoury dish that is commonly found in food centres across Singapore and Malaysia, this popular favourite is given a spicy kick with the addition of chilli slices, and a pleasant tang with a dash of lime.

INGREDIENTS

Boneless fish fillet (seabass or mackerel)	800 g (1 ³/₄ lb)
Corn flour (cornstarch)	2 Tbsp
Salt	a pinch + more for seasoning
Sesame oil	1 Tbsp
Shallots	2, peeled and finely sliced
Garlic	2 cloves, peeled and minced
Red chilli	1, finely sliced
Light soy sauce	1 Tbsp
Lime juice	from 1 lime
Water	750 ml (24 fl oz / 3 cups)
Egg noodles	400 g (14 oz)
Spring onions (scallions)	a small bunch

METHOD

- In a blender, process fish fillet with corn flour and a pinch of salt to form a paste.

- Using wet, clean hands, roll and knead fish paste until slightly elastic. Form fishballs of desired size.

- Cook fishballs in hot boiling water. Remove from heat and set aside.

- Heat sesame oil in a casserole or pan. Sauté shallots, garlic and chilli until fragrant.

- Add soy sauce and lime juice, followed by water.

- Add noodles and fishballs.

- Simmer on low heat and season with salt.

- Once noodles are cooked, garnish with spring onions.

- Remove from heat and serve immediately.

chicken quinoa with vegetables Serves 4

Quinoa is a seed that can be cooked like whole grains such as rice and barley. It is low in fat and is a popular choice among the health-conscious. Quinoa is found to be able to prevent stroke, hypertension and heart diseases.

INGREDIENTS

Quinoa	2 cups
Water	1 litre (32 fl oz / 4 cups)
Salt	to taste
Extra virgin olive oil	3 Tbsp
Cumin seeds	1 Tbsp
Garlic	3 cloves, peeled and minced
Red onion	1, peeled and quartered
Shallots	2, peeled and sliced
Chicken breast fillet	300 g (10$^1/_2$ oz), cubed
Eggplant (aubergine/ brinjal)	1, large
Red pepper (capsicum)	1, cubed
Carrot	1, diced
Tomatoes	2, quartered
Tomato purée	1 Tbsp
Paprika	1 Tbsp
Passata (see page 67)	200 ml (6$^3/_4$ fl oz)
Italian seasoning	1 Tbsp
Kosher salt	1 tsp
Ground black pepper	to taste
Lemon juice	from 1 lemon
Parsley	a few sprigs, chopped

NOTE

Passata is a more liquid form of tomato purée, which is chunkier and gives a different texture to the food.

METHOD

• Boil quinoa with water and salt in a rice cooker. Alternatively, cook quinoa in a regular pot. When tender and ready, fluff with a fork.

• Heat olive oil in a wok and sauté cumin seeds, garlic, onion and shallots until fragrant.

• Add chicken and cook until meat is almost brown.

- Add eggplant, red pepper, carrot, quartered tomatoes, tomato purée and paprika.
- After a few minutes, add passata, Italian seasoning, kosher salt, black pepper, lemon juice and parsley.
- Simmer on low heat until gravy has thickened and chicken is tender.
- Add cooked quinoa and mix well. Serve warm.

seabass pais Serves 4

Seabass is rich in omega-3 fatty acids. Its flavour is enhanced with spices and coconut in this traditional Asian recipe.

INGREDIENTS

Whole seabass	1, large, cleaned
Turmeric	1 tsp
Grated coconut	4 Tbsp
Dried red chillies	5, soaked in hot water until soft
Shallots	5, peeled and sliced
Garlic	2 cloves, peeled
Ginger	2.5-cm (1-in) knob, peeled
Galangal (*lengkuas*)	2.5-cm (1-in) knob, peeled
Tamarind paste	1 Tbsp
Lemon grass	1 stalk, shredded
Water	as needed
Canola oil	1 tsp
Red onion	1, large, peeled and sliced
Tomatoes	2, chopped
Salt	$1/4$ tsp
Aluminium foil or banana leaf	for wrapping
Lemon juice	from 1 lemon

NOTE
If using banana leaf, wash and scald it with hot water, then wipe dry before using.

METHOD

- Marinate seabass with turmeric and set aside.
- In a wok, dry-roast coconut without oil until it becomes golden brown.
- In a blender, process coconut with chillies, shallots, garlic, ginger, galangal, tamarind and lemon grass to form a thick paste, adding water as needed.
- Preheat oven to 180°C (350°F).
- Heat oil in a wok and sauté red onion slices briefly. Set aside.
- Using the same oil, temper blended spices until the oil splutters. Add chopped tomatoes and salt, then remove from heat.

- Place half of the spice paste on an aluminium foil or banana leaf that is big enough for wrapping the fish. Place seabass over the spices. Cover seabass with remaining spice paste and garnish with sautéed onion slices.

- Fold edges of aluminium foil, or secure the edges of banana leaf with toothpicks to enclose the fish. Bake for 30 minutes.

- Drizzle lemon juice over the fish and serve immediately.

weights and measures

Quantities for this book are given in Metric, Imperial and American (spoon and cup) measures. Standard spoon and cup measurements used are: 1 tsp = 5 ml, 1 Tbsp = 15 ml, 1 cup = 250 ml. All measures are level unless otherwise stated.

Liquid And Volume Measures

Metric	Imperial	American
5 ml	1/6 fl oz	1 teaspoon
10 ml	1/3 fl oz	1 dessertspoon
15 ml	1/2 fl oz	1 tablespoon
60 ml	2 fl oz	1/4 cup (4 tablespoons)
85 ml	2 1/2 fl oz	1/3 cup
90 ml	3 fl oz	3/8 cup (6 tablespoons)
125 ml	4 fl oz	1/2 cup
180 ml	6 fl oz	3/4 cup
250 ml	8 fl oz	1 cup
300 ml	10 fl oz (1/2 pint)	1 1/4 cups
375 ml	12 fl oz	1 1/2 cups
435 ml	14 fl oz	1 3/4 cups
500 ml	16 fl oz	2 cups
625 ml	20 fl oz (1 pint)	2 1/2 cups
750 ml	24 fl oz (1 1/5 pints)	3 cups
1 litre	32 fl oz (1 3/5 pints)	4 cups
1.25 litres	40 fl oz (2 pints)	5 cups
1.5 litres	48 fl oz (2 2/5 pints)	6 cups
2.5 litres	80 fl oz (4 pints)	10 cups

Dry Measures

Metric	Imperial
30 grams	1 ounce
45 grams	1 1/2 ounces
55 grams	2 ounces
70 grams	2 1/2 ounces
85 grams	3 ounces
100 grams	3 1/2 ounces
110 grams	4 ounces
125 grams	4 1/2 ounces
140 grams	5 ounces
280 grams	10 ounces
450 grams	16 ounces (1 pound)
500 grams	1 pound, 1 1/2 ounces
700 grams	1 1/2 pounds
800 grams	1 3/4 pounds
1 kilogram	2 pounds, 3 ounces
1.5 kilograms	3 pounds, 4 1/2 ounces
2 kilograms	4 pounds, 6 ounces

Length

Metric	Imperial
0.5 cm	1/4 inch
1 cm	1/2 inch
1.5 cm	3/4 inch
2.5 cm	1 inch

Oven Temperature

	°C	°F	Gas Regulo
Very slow	120	250	1
Slow	150	300	2
Moderately slow	160	325	3
Moderate	180	350	4
Moderately hot	190/200	375/400	5/6
Hot	210/220	410/425	6/7
Very hot	230	450	8
Super hot	250/290	475/550	9/10

Abbreviation

tsp	teaspoon
Tbsp	tablespoon
g	gram
kg	kilogram
ml	millilitre